Original title:
The Jewelry of the Soul

Copyright © 2025 Creative Arts Management OÜ
All rights reserved.

Author: Harris Montgomery
ISBN HARDBACK: 978-1-80586-078-5
ISBN PAPERBACK: 978-1-80586-550-6

Ciphers in Light

In the attic, a box full of strange things,
Sparkling socks and a hat with wings.
A necklace made of gummy bears,
From a party—what fun! Who even cares?

With mismatched earrings that jingle and clash,
One's a button, the other's a piece of trash.
I wear them proudly, a sight to behold,
A fashion statement that never gets old.

A ring shaped like a pretzel, how neat!
Dancing around on my wobbly feet.
I twirl in circles, the world is a blur,
Who needs a crown when you've got a slur?

In the mirror, my trinkets shine bright,
Every oddity a source of delight.
Laughing with friends, we share silly tales,
Of treasures we find in our whimsical trails.

The Tapestry of Essence

In a world of sparkly dreams,
Even socks can wear some gleams.
A clumsy dance, a glitzy fall,
Who said we need to stand up tall?

Laughter shines like diamond dust,
In mismatched shoes, we jest, we trust.
With silly hats and paints a-flair,
There's bling in living without a care.

Golden Echoes

Echoes of laughter, bright as gold,
In Grandma's stories, the quirks unfold.
Her necklace jingles, so does her grin,
She says, 'You're charming when you spin!'

A quirky dance at Sunday brunch,
With jellybeans that pack a punch.
In heart-shaped frames, we capture fun,
Each moment's jewel when day is done.

Shimmering Truths

Truths are like gems, they cut and shine,
Especially when mixed with quirky wine.
A wink and a nod, the grin's not a lie,
We sparkle brighter, just you and I.

In silly poses, we find our flair,
With bow ties made from Grandma's hair.
A truth so sweet, no need for prude,
Life's shimmering truths are often crude!

Polished Serenity

Serenity's a polished rock,
That rolls away with every clock.
In slippers bright and mismatched socks,
We find our peace in silly flocks.

The laughter flows like rivers wide,
In wobbly boats, we take the ride.
With every giggle, we find a song,
In polished life, we all belong.

Celestial Embellishments

Stars wear gowns of sparkly dust,
Planets prance, they simply must.
Comets with glittery tails so long,
Dance around like they belong.

Moonbeams tease with silver winks,
Galaxies laugh, or so one thinks.
With cosmic jokes on a shimmering stage,
They twirl and giggle, year after age.

The Art of Radiance

Sunshine drapes in golden sheets,
Tickling flowers with warm tweets.
Rainbow ribbons in the sky,
Play hopscotch, oh my, oh my!

Glittery breezes swirl around,
Nature's snickers, a playful sound.
With every twirl of light and hue,
It's a joyous merry-go-round for you!

Inner Riches

A heart adorned with laughter rings,
Jokes and giggles are fancy things.
Within the mind, gems brightly shine,
Crafted from memories, oh so fine!

Thoughts like pearls, with wisdom's glow,
Funny quirks, like a circus show.
Treasure chests filled with cheer so bold,
Who knew riches were made of gold?

Luminescent Pathways

Witty whispers light the way,
Follow the giggles, come what may.
Every step shines with delight,
Dancing shadows in the night.

Starlit signs and moonbeam trails,
Lead to laughter, never fails.
With every chuckle, each step's a thrill,
Life's funny paths, a comedy drill!

Whispers of Inner Splendor

In the attic of my thoughts so bright,
Sparkles dance in the middle of the night.
A tiara made of spaghetti strands,
With meatballs as diamonds, oh how it stands!

A necklace of laughter, cheerful and round,
Worn proudly as silly as it is profound.
Charmed by the folly of life's little games,
I strut like a peacock, shouting my names!

Elegance of the Mind

A bow tie made of belief and delight,
Confidence glowing, oh what a sight!
Top hat of wonder, tipped just so,
My thoughts play jazz like a musical show!

Cufflinks of giggles, every joke on cue,
I step forth in style, a grand debut.
With twirls and spins 'round the mental spree,
How dapper I feel being truly me!

Charms of the Heartstrings

A brooch of jokes pinned close to my heart,
Winking and blinking, playing its part.
Bracelets of kindness jingling in tune,
Under the light of a goofy balloon!

Earrings of stories, each one a thrill,
Whisper secrets of laughter, what a skill!
Adorned in the glow of pure joyful bliss,
Life's a comedy, can't let this chance miss!

Ornamented Dreams

Dreams glitter like stars, caught in a net,
I wear them like crowns, none I regret.
Broaches of ambitions with a hefty dose,
Silly wishes riding on dreams like a carousel close!

Each fantasy shines, a poke at the real,
Crazy and quirky, they dance and they wheel.
With each little whim, I scribble my fate,
A tapestry woven in giggles and quakes!

Artifacts of Affection

In the attic, memories lay,
Dusty trinkets, come what may.
A rubber duck, a broken toy,
Giggles whisper, purest joy.

A locket shaped like a cat,
Worn by grandpa, imagine that!
A spoon that sings, or so they say,
It dances when there's food on the tray.

A hat that talks of summer days,
With jokes that turn the sun ablaze.
A garden gnome with winking eyes,
Sprinkling laughter in disguise.

So treasure these odd little things,
For joy is found in what it brings.
Each artifact, a tale to spin,
In the heart, where chuckles begin.

Pearls of Wisdom

In a clam, there lies a gem,
A wise old crustacean's diadem.
He teaches lessons filled with fun,
Like don't leave home without your bun.

A fish swims by with glasses neat,
Says, "Ninety percent's just being sweet!"
With every bubble, wisdom flies,
While all the anemones just sighs.

From every shell, a secret spills,
Of sandy shores and ocean thrills.
Laughing waves, they churn and dance,
Whispering wisdom with a glance.

So pick a pearl from the beach of fate,
Wear it proudly, it's never too late.
For wisdom is but a silly jest,
Wrapped in laughter, it's truly blessed.

The Tapestry of Inner Light

Weaving threads of joy and cheer,
A funky tapestry, oh dear!
With colors bright and patterns wild,
Each stitch reflects the inner child.

A patch of giggles, a splash of glee,
A doodle here of cheeky spree.
Stitched with love and silly flair,
It tells a tale beyond compare.

In every knot, a secret shared,
Of silly pranks and joys declared.
A burst of colors, a snickered tale,
Each piece a memory, light as a sail.

So wrap it round when days feel gray,
This tapestry brightens every way.
A fabric spun from hugs and smiles,
Woven together through humorous styles.

Trinkets of the Spirit

A feather found, a silly grin,
Hold it close, let the fun begin.
A pebble painted with a smile,
Each trinket tells a story worthwhile.

A bell that jingles with delight,
Announces joy, both day and night.
A bottle filled with summer air,
Open it up, and dance without a care.

A scribbled note from days of old,
"Don't take life too seriously," it told.
With every trinket that you find,
A giggle lingers, all combined.

So treasure these oddities bright,
They spark joy and banish fright.
For in the spirit's playful dance,
Every trinket holds a chance.

Dazzling Inner Light

In the depths of my quirky mind,
Fashion gems I try to find.
A diamond made of silly dreams,
Sparkling with my laughter's beams.

Jesters wear crowns of paper clips,
Twinkling in their playful quips.
With every grin, my treasures shine,
Glitters from this goofy line.

The Crown of Whispers

Upon my head a crown of jest,
Made of chocolate, it's the best!
A candy jewel, it gleams so sweet,
With every bite, my joy's complete.

Whispers dance in glitter's glow,
Tickling my thoughts, just like a show.
A laugh, a giggle, gems of cheer,
Make my crown the one they fear!

Echoes of the Heart's Delicacy

My heart's a funny little store,
Filled with giggles, not a bore.
Each echo filled with silly tunes,
Swaying under crescent moons.

Delicate whispers, sweet and bright,
Bouncing back with pure delight.
Each note, a spark of brightened fun,
In this bazaar, I'm number one!

Luminescent Thoughts

Shiny ideas bounce around,
Like disco balls that spin and sound.
Glowing thoughts just can't stay still,
Tickling my mind, what a thrill!

Each twist and turn leads to a smile,
Radiating light all the while.
Illuminated, I prance and sway,
Crafting joy in a luminous way.

Radiant Whispers

In the mirror, my hair's a mess,
Hiding treasures, I must confess.
Oh, the nonsense that I find,
A spoon, a sock, my cat, so unkind.

A laughter bubbling up so bright,
My pearls are peas, what a silly sight!
Each glimmer shines with a story spun,
Even if it's all just flimsy fun.

Enchanted Charms

A bracelet made of gummy bears,
Worn at parties, brings out stares.
My earrings? Buttons from a coat,
Dancing lightly, they make me float.

A necklace of my childhood dreams,
Composed of ice cream and whipped cream.
With every jingle, every clink,
They make me laugh, they make me wink.

The Adornment of Existence

I wear a crown of paperclips,
As if I'm queen of laughing quips.
My jewels, shiny paper stars,
Representing all my silly scars.

With every step, a jingle sings,
A reminder, life's a dance with flings.
Though mismatched and a bit absurd,
Each trinket tells a tale unheard.

Soul Stones

Rock and roll, with pebbles in hand,
Each one a gem from laughter's band.
Stones that sparkle, like jokes unsaid,
That keep us chuckling, even in bed.

A collection of quirks, all piled high,
Mix-ups and giggles, oh me, oh my!
With every glance at this playful stash,
It's hard not to smile, it's a joyful clash.

Radiance Within

A smile like diamonds, shining bright,
Thoughts like pearls, a pure delight.
With every giggle, a gem appears,
Laughter wraps us, more than mere cheers.

In a world of chaos, we find some gold,
Stories and wonders, never get old.
Dance like rubies, skip like a star,
Showing our quirks, that's how we are!

Echoes of Elegance

The clanking of laughter, oh what a sound,
As we jingle and giggle, we wear joy around.
Witty banter, a bracelet we weave,
Each line a charm, who would believe?

In a spiffy coat made of cracks and quirks,
We flaunt our oddities, that's how it works.
With whimsical thoughts in a sparkling array,
We dress our souls in humor each day!

Sparkling Reflections

In a mirror of jokes, how we shine,
Each punchline of life, a twist so divine.
With each saucy wink, the sparkle ignites,
We gather our glimmers in festive delights.

Twinkling in mischief, like emerald eyes,
A cackle of joy, our ultimate prize.
We dance like the stars on a silvery night,
Our spirits adorned, what a marvelous sight!

Ornaments of Being

Beneath silly hats and outrageous ties,
Are treasures of laughter in clever disguise.
We adorn our hearts with the quirkiest trends,
In the gallery of life, humor transcends.

With flip-flop wisdom and sock puppet dreams,
Each moment's a jewel, bursting at the seams.
We wear our oddities like crowns of gold,
In this whimsical world, let the laughter unfold!

Crystals of Connection

In a world where jokes unite,
Crystals twinkle, oh so bright.
Laughter's sparkle in the air,
Mismatched socks, a fashion dare.

Bubbly vibes in every room,
Friendship's glow, like springtime bloom.
Gems of laughter, rich and rare,
Silly faces, hearts laid bare.

With each giggle, bonds are tied,
Witty words, the joy we ride.
Like magnets made of happy thoughts,
Togetherness we're never caught.

So let's adorn our souls with cheer,
Jokes and pranks that disappear.
In this treasure, pure delight,
Crystals shining, day and night.

Luminescence of Dreams

In the land where dreams do dance,
Funny hats, they take a chance.
Glow-in-the-dark, our wishes beam,
Silly thoughts enough to dream.

We chase the stars like little kids,
Wearing smiles, we flip the lids.
Mirror balls and sparkly schemes,
Our playful hearts, the brightest beams.

Dreams are gems that make us grin,
Chasing them, let giggles spin.
From the depths of each sweet night,
Laughter glows, a pure delight.

So paint the sky with colors bright,
Every blink, a laugh ignites.
In this realm of joy, we fly,
With dreams like stars up in the sky.

The Essence Embellished

With a wink, we sprinkle cheer,
Essence of silliness is near.
Giggles wrap around our hearts,
Dressing life in funny parts.

Embellished souls in dance and play,
Wearing mischief every day.
Like confetti thrown for fun,
Joyful chaos has begun.

A dash of laughter, a pinch of tease,
Life's a game, do as you please.
Bright ideas, like bubbles, soar,
In this essence, we explore.

So come and join this jolly ride,
With smiles wide, let's cast aside.
Every moment's a gem that's bright,
Embroidered in love's pure light.

Trinkets of Time

Time ticks by with a silly rhyme,
Crafting trinkets in the climb.
Jokes as badges on our chest,
In the laughter, we are blessed.

Chasing moments, swift and light,
Wobbling like a duck in flight.
Each second wrapped in golden threads,
Ticklish tales and funny spreads.

Memories like shiny beads,
Filled with love and goofy deeds.
Tales of mischief we will share,
Trinkets of time, beyond compare.

Celebrate each twist and turn,
In this dance, we'll laugh and learn.
With every tick, what joy we find,
In the treasures of loving minds.

The Allure of Existence

Life's a quirky gem, I've found,
With laughter wrapped around,
I wear socks that never match,
And dance like a silly patch.

Every day's a shiny quest,
For the quirkiest little jest,
I misplace my keys so grand,
And trip on air, just as I planned.

My friends twinkle like bright stars,
In coffee shops and passing cars,
We giggle at the silliest things,
Creating joy that truly sings.

So treasure life's amusing twist,
In every laugh, we coexist,
A sparkle here, a wink or two,
In this raucous life, we break through.

A Dance of Radiance

I twirl like a disco ball,
In a dazzling, giggly sprawl,
My feet find rhythm in the night,
As I trip on my own delight.

When life brings awkward charm around,
I wiggle like I've just been crowned,
And laughter fills the sparkling air,
With friends who join this merry flair.

Each stumble's just a chance to shine,
In this grand dance, I'm feeling fine,
The world's a stage, absurd, pristine,
With twinkling lights, a vibrant scene.

So let's embrace the silly sway,
And giggle all our blues away,
In every misstep, joy does prance,
Creating brilliance in our dance.

Lines of Luster

In crooked lines, we find our groove,
With laughter that's the perfect move,
Each blunder just a gleaming thread,
That weaves through life, light-heartedly spread.

Our stories sparkle, every twist,
In moments that we can't resist,
Witty quips and jests are grand,
Creating gems that can withstand.

When life throws us a curveball tight,
We juggle it with pure delight,
Like misfit diamonds on parade,
Breaking norms, unafraid.

So here's to laughter, bright and bold,
The quirkiest tales yet to be told,
In each line shines a silly gleam,
Together we compose a dream.

Fragments of Brilliance

In tiny bits, our lives are spun,
With glitter trails and lots of fun,
We collect the laughs like precious stones,
In silly patterns, never alone.

Each moment's a fragment, bold and free,
In the scrapbook of our memory,
From ice cream spills to giggling fits,
Designs of joy in quirky bits.

With eccentric tales that brightly beam,
Our friendships glimmer, like a dream,
Over spilled drinks and forgotten fries,
We find our spark in the surprise.

So dance through life, embrace each piece,
With laughter that will never cease,
In every fragment, pure delight,
We shine together, oh so bright.

Glimmers of the Unseen

In pockets deep where secrets lie,
A missing sock, oh me, oh my!
Nuggets of gold, or silly delight,
A rubber band wrapped up tight.

Who knew that lint could shine so bright?
The crumbs of joy, a tasty bite.
With every waddle, a jiggle, a grin,
A treasure trove found within my skin!

Wear your quirks like a crown today,
Socks that clash? Let them play!
For laughter's jewels, they dance and spin,
Polished by love and where we've been.

In every giggle, in every sigh,
The brightest gems you'll ever spy.
With heart and humor, we load our tool,
Each day adorned—who's the fool?

Echoes of Celestial Beauty

Stars wear coats of shimmering dust,
But Auntie Edna? She's a must!
With beads from her youth, she jangles and sighs,
Tales of mischief float up to the skies.

In the fridge, a gift from a cosmic meal,
Leftover cake—an interstellar deal!
The planets align for a holiday feast,
Where calories vanish, and laughter's released.

Her pearls of wisdom, a hoot to behold,
As she recounts tales the poets told.
In each sweet story, joy does bloom,
Sprinkling stardust all over the room.

With every giggle, we reach for the stars,
Counting the treasures we've packed in jars.
Between the raindrops and moonlit trails,
The echoes of beauty forever prevails.

The Lustrous Essence

Amidst the chaos of dishes piled high,
Lurking leaves a twinkle, oh me, oh my!
Remnants of pizza? A lunch with a twist,
In culinary wonders, it's hard to resist!

Juggling mismatched socks, a pair on the run,
Funky patterns make laundry feel fun.
With each sock lost, a giggle we find,
In the essence of life, no fabric is blind.

Tiny orbs of wisdom, wisdom so bright,
Float in our coffee—what a delight!
Stirring up laughter with every sip,
Sip twice for treasures—let joy be the trip!

Who needs diamonds when we've got this tale?
With inside jokes that never grow stale.
Wearing laughter like a badge on our sleeve,
In this dance of light, we truly believe!

Trinkets of Truth

Beneath the couch, where dust bunnies dwell,
Lies a treasure chest—oh, what a swell!
With crayons, lost change, and half a stick gum,
In the land of forgotten, we find our fun!

Cracked screen savers and jokes made of cheese,
Laughter spills over like a summer breeze.
With each silly moment, we gather our gems,
Jokes that outshine the most precious diadems.

Collecting weird trinkets, odd bits, and bobs,
In the fabric of life, we craft our own jobs.
Each selfie a jewel, a sparkle, a grin,
In the portrait of truth, we find where we've been.

So wear your quirks with unfettered pride,
For in these small things, our souls will abide.
Cuz laughter's the charm that won't ever fade,
In this treasure hunt, let's dance unafraid!

Inner Sparkles

In the depths of my quirky heart,
Glitters of laughter play their part.
A hiccup of joy, a twinkling grin,
Each giggle, a treasure hiding within.

With every chuckle, a shimmer appears,
A sparkle of mischief, laughter, and cheers.
In my pockets, I keep all the fun,
Like a squirrel storing gems from the sun.

Oh, how I dance with absurd delight,
Jiving like stars in a comical night.
With winks and jests, the show goes on,
My heart's a carnival, where no one's drawn.

So wear your quirks, let your giggles show,
For inner sparkles make silly hearts glow.

Threads of Brilliance

In tangled yarns of laughter spun,
I weave my puns, twirl 'til I'm done.
Each joke a stitch, a witty design,
Draped in humor, so divine.

Noodle arm and disco feet,
A fashion show where bloopers meet.
I strut the runway, a jester bold,
In threads of brilliance, carefree and uncontrolled.

With every twist, I catch a smile,
My funky outfit, oh so versatile!
A hat made of giggles, mismatched with flair,
I'm the portrait of chaos, but who would care?

So let's all wear our laughter proudly,
In threads of brilliance, let's get rowdy!

Dazzling Dreams

In my dreamy land where sillies loom,
I ride on unicorns that burst with perfume.
Each laugh a balloon that floats to the sky,
While cookies rain down, oh my, oh my!

Napping on clouds of cotton candy,
I'm the queen of whimsy, isn't it dandy?
A crown of gumdrops atop my head,
I prance through dreams, never a shred.

In this realm, reality takes a snooze,
Where even the grumpy are tickled and choose.
To dance with the daisies, a silly parade,
Our dazzling dreams, unashamedly displayed.

So twirl with me in this dreamscape bright,
And let's dazzle the world, with pure delight!

Charmed Reflections

In the mirror, what do I see?
A jester's grin staring back at me.
With a wink and a giggle, I strike a pose,
Charm wrapped in laughter, that's how it goes.

A dance of shadows from my silly hat,
Reflections sparkle, imagine that!
With every turn, a chuckle flows,
Shimmering tales only silliness knows.

So here's to charm in every blunder,
To finding joy in life's funny thunder.
Mirror, mirror, let the fun unfurl,
For in these reflections, I'm a glorious swirl!

With each glance, may laughter reign,
In charmed reflections, break the mundane!

Tokens of Love's Craft

A locket shaped like a doughnut,
Holds memories of my last brunch.
Sparkling gems of laughter,
In my heart they always crunch.

Bracelets made of silly string,
Clink and clank as I dance.
Each charm a funny fling,
In this love, I take a chance.

An earring shaped like a cat,
Whispers softly in my ear.
Purring sweetly, imagine that,
A feline joke I love to hear.

Rings that twirl and spin about,
With glitter that just won't quit.
Each piece I cannot live without,
In my heart they truly sit.

The Splendor Within

A crown of dandelion fluff,
Sits upon my dreamy head.
Its majestic, silly stuff,
Makes every worry turn to bread.

Necklaces of licorice lace,
Twisted sweet, oh what a treat.
Happiness weaves a sturdy base,
For dancing to a silly beat.

An anklet made from candy chains,
With every step, it squeaks and slips.
The taste of joy within it reigns,
As laughter tumbles from my lips.

In this treasure chest I find,
Tokens of a life well-played.
My joy, a spark of the divine,
In my foolishness displayed.

The Glistening Core

A gem like jelly, wobbly bright,
Shimmers in the morning sun.
I giggle hard, what a sight,
A delight that's full of fun!

Brooches made of rubber bands,
Colorful and stretched with glee.
Worn with grace, no one understands,
This zest for life, wild and free.

Earrings that dangle like dreams,
Vibrant hues dance with my mood.
In the laughter, joy redeems,
A treasure that's so very good.

The glistening core of who I am,
Is stitched together with a joke.
A tapestry of playful glam,
In every moment, laughter spoke.

Echoes of Timeless Beauty

A ring that jingles when I laugh,
Echoes down the corridor.
With every ding, it's a sweet gaffe,
A reminder of joy at my core.

Necklaces of spaghettini,
A dish that keeps on giving.
Their twisty forms look quite silly,
Yet that's just how I am living!

Each charm a quirk, each tale a tease,
A patchwork of delightful grace.
The laughter flows like a gentle breeze,
Painting smiles on every face.

In this world of playful gems,
The echoes linger, always near.
Crafted from the whimsical stems,
Of love's laughter, loud and clear.

Unseen Opulence

In the attic, dust bunnies hide,
Old treasures piled up, love and pride.
A sock with a hole, a vintage toy,
Turns ordinary laughs into pure joy.

A spoon that once stirred sweet apple pie,
Declares, 'Don't worry, just ask why!'
Each quirky find, a giggle or two,
Unseen riches make the world feel new.

Oh, that button, a jewel in disguise,
Hiding stories behind its round eyes.
With every blink, it whispers a tale,
Of fashion faux pas and a pirate sail.

So gather your treasures, each knick-knack bright,
In the laughter of memories, all feels right.
Who needs gold chains that sparkle and gleam?
When silly old treasures can ignite a dream!

Glowing Memories

A jellybean jar, a monument sweet,
Holds precious moments, a tasty treat.
With each little bite, nostalgia ignites,
As we reminisce on long-ago nights.

Stained glass windows of thoughts in our heads,
Reflecting the joys like unmade beds.
The glow of a smile, the warmth of a friend,
In this candy-coated world, laughter won't end.

A dance on the fridge, magnets aligned,
Reveal laughter echoes, silliness entwined.
Each note of a song, a melody spun,
Turns mundane chores into great deals of fun.

So toast to the moments, funny and bright,
Like fireflies flashing, a whimsical sight.
In the glow of our hearts, mischief holds sway,
Yet memories shine in their own zany way!

Treasure Troves of Thought

Under every hat lies a secret or two,
An idea or whimsy, a cosmic 'who knew?'
Like lost pirate maps with a treasure to find,
Thoughts linger like jelly stuck deep in your mind.

A shoebox of giggles, a bucket of fun,
Who knew socks could sparkle under the sun?
Each thought is a gem waiting to shine,
In the treasure trove of your own quirky mind.

A light bulb flickers, inventiveness flows,
What's that? A duck wearing rollerblade shoes?
Such nonsense unlocks a pathway to glee,
Bringing absurdity forth like a wild jubilee!

So delve into laughter, into whimsy dive,
In this treasure trove, we are most alive.
The riches of mirth aren't counted in gold,
But in stories and chuckles forever retold!

Whispers of the Heart

An odd pair of mittens sits lonely on shelves,
Whispering secrets, they know themselves.
In laughter they chatter, recalling the days,
When snowball fights ruled and chilled winter play.

A mismatched sock tells tales of a race,
With dancing feet trying to keep up the pace.
Each trip on a shoelace sends giggles around,
As stories of clumsiness grace the ground.

Balloons in the attic, deflated but bold,
Swirl with their secrets, stories untold.
In their silent giggles, we find a refrain,
Of parties unplanned and celebrating the mundane.

So tune in to whispers, let laughter ignite,
In the awkward and silly, the heart takes flight.
Each moment a jewel, a jest here or there,
Turns mundane existence into a carnival fair!

Reflections of Joy

In mirrors of laughter, we often gaze,
Discovering quirks in our silly ways.
With every chuckle, we shine a bit bright,
Twinkling in jest, like stars in the night.

Our hearts wear smiles like hats on a cat,
Each goofy moment, a whimsical spat.
In the sparkle of giggles, we find our tune,
Dancing like fireflies beneath the full moon.

When life hands you lemons, just juggle away,
Make candy out of stress, brighten your day.
With friends by our side, who needs to be wise?
Our joy's a parade, a masquerade of ties.

So let's string together these moments so sweet,
With laughter and light, we'll never admit defeat.
In the tapestry woven with threads bold and bright,
We find joy's reflections, our playful delight.

Beads of Serenity

Like marbles of calm in a jumbled purse,
Each day a new finding, for better or worse.
A bead of a grin, a chuckle or two,
In the chaos of life, we find our own clue.

We gather our wisdom like pebbles in sand,
Finding peace in the quirks that life has planned.
With every odd thought, a treasure to keep,
Funny how laughter can silence the steep.

The world's a big tapestry, patchworked with glee,
Each knot tells a story, just wait and see.
With a wink and a nudge, we'll weave and we'll play,
Creating a peace that won't fade away.

So toast to the moments, so light and so free,
In beads of delight, we find harmony.
Life's a quirky dance, a comedian's dream,
In the stillness of joy, we twirl and we beam.

Luminous Echoes

In the corridors of laughter, echoes ring clear,
Like whispers of sunshine that tickle the ear.
Every joke crafted with love and delight,
Leaves trails of bright giggles that dance in the night.

We glide on our dreams like shoes two sizes too big,
Wobbling around, oh, what a fine jig!
Each twinkle a memory, bright as a flame,
Like fireflies buzzing, none will be the same.

Through comedy's lens, life's moments we weave,
On the stage of existence, we constantly cleave.
With laughter our language, we'll conquer the strife,
In luminous echoes, we celebrate life.

So let's raise a toast to the hapless and bold,
To the funny stories that never grow old.
In the theater of joy, we dance and we sing,
Finding light in the laughter that each moment can bring.

Attributes of the Inner Flame

What sparks within us, so bright and so funny,
Turns life's little troubles into sweet soothing honey.
Each giggle's a flicker, each chuckle a cheer,
Lighting the shadows that linger near.

Our quirks are a gift wrapped in laughter and jest,
With hugs of joy that make every day blessed.
When humor ignites, it's a glorious show,
Attributes shining, like stars in a row.

Let's dance with our blunders, twirl with our flaws,
In the comedy of life, deliver our applause.
With a wink and a nod, we'll pet our own shame,
For the funniest tales are the ones without blame.

So let's kindle the flame, let frivolity reign,
In the attributes of humor, we find joy's domain.
Here's to the blunders, the giggles, the charm,
In the warmth of our banter, we are safe from all harm.

Heartstrings and Jewels

In a drawer, I found a ring,
So shiny, it made the toaster sing.
It promised love but was just a joke,
A broken clasp and a funny bloke.

A necklace made of paper clips,
Worn to fancy dinners with pure fun trips.
Friends all laughed, 'What a sight!'
I claimed I was a fashion highlight.

With earrings shaped like tiny fries,
Who needs gold when laughter flies?
Each clink and clatter brings delight,
As I strut around like I own the night.

So wear your quirks, let fun unfurl,
For genuine gems may make you swirl.
A silly heart holds such weight,
It's better than gold, now that's first-rate!

Traces of Treasure

Found a locket with a picture of soup,
Thought it was treasure—a real fashion scoop!
The kids all giggled, 'What's your style?'
I winked and said, 'It's worth the while.'

A brooch of a cat with a silly grin,
Clipped it to my hat—let the fun begin!
We paraded down the street so proud,
Meowing and laughing, drawing a crowd.

Rubies made of jelly beans so sweet,
Adorning my toes while I dance on the street.
Passersby burst into contagious laughter,
Who knew goofiness could be such a factor?

Oh, these artifacts from my wacky quest,
Bring joy and giggles—life's a jest!
For in every trinket lies a tale,
Let's celebrate humor; let's set sail!

Ethereal Adornments

A crown made of tin foil, sparkly bright,
Wore it while cooking; it was quite a sight!
Neighbors peeking, 'What's going on?'
I said, 'Just bling while I bake my scone!'

Bracelets crafted from gummy bears,
Snacking while sharing laughs and cares.
'It's a gourmet style,' I boldly said,
Tasting each gem before they fled.

A belt of spoons, quite a fine flair,
Every clang adds rhythm to the air.
I danced with joy, a kitchen ballet,
Making my own fun in a comical way.

So let the oddities be your art,
With silliness, fashion plays the part.
For true flair comes from a joyful heart,
In our bizarre world, we're all off the chart!

Echoes of the Heart

With a string from my old guitar,
I fashioned a bracelet; oh, how bizarre!
Each strum brings giggles, every glance a cheer,
When I wear it proudly, it's music to the ear.

An ankle bracelet made of candy wraps,
Dancing around, I take funny laps.
Sweetness falling with each silly twirl,
Who knew my legs could bring such a whirl?

Peculiar pendants stuck on my coat,
A mix of buttons, each tells a note.
With stories linked, we laugh and connect,
Fashion's a joke—but oh, the respect!

So toss aside those normals and norms,
Wear the odd, embrace all the forms.
With laughter as the cornerstone of art,
We truly shine when we play from the heart!

Whispered Charms

In a corner, dreams take flight,
Sparkling like stars in the night.
Chains of laughter, tangled glee,
Jokes that shimmer, wild and free.

Witty whispers float in air,
A treasure chest without a care.
With each chuckle, a gem appears,
Polished by our happy tears.

Funny faces, stories grand,
Each moment, simply unplanned.
A necklace strung with silly times,
Adorned by all our playful rhymes.

Laughter rings like precious bells,
Echoing tales; oh, how it swells!
In every jest, a twinkle finds,
A charm that dances in our minds.

The Gilded Heart

Beating bright with pure delight,
Shiny jokes, oh, what a sight!
A heart adorned with giggles loud,
A zany spirit, oh so proud.

Wrapped in glitter, love entwined,
Eccentric thoughts, whimsically aligned.
With every grin, a sparkle spread,
Gilded dreams dance in my head.

Banter soft, like velvet's caress,
Silly moments, no need to impress.
With every quirk, my soul aglow,
A loved-up heart, just letting go.

Laughter bubbles like fine champagne,
The shine of joy, never in vain.
In this warmth, we gently twine,
Crafting moments, pure divine.

Inner Glow

In the depths, a flicker hangs,
A beacon bright as laughter sang.
Glowing thoughts, a lantern's light,
Ticklish tales spark pure delight.

Brightening days with silly schemes,
Quirky wishes, chasing dreams.
Each giggle a radiant thread,
Stitching joy where darkness tread.

Flashes of fun, like shooting stars,
Warming hearts, no need for cars.
In each chuckle lies a glow,
An inner rush that steals the show.

A hearty laugh can lift a frown,
Draped in smiles, I wear my crown.
Glorious sparks, we take our stance,
Shining bright, in joyful dance.

Mosaic of Memories

Pieces scattered, bright and bold,
A patchwork quilt of tales retold.
Every moment, a vibrant hue,
Crafting joy in all we do.

Breaks of laughter, shades of cheer,
Mosaics formed by love sincere.
In every crack, a giggle lays,
Reflecting joy in countless ways.

With a wink, the world unfolds,
Stories stitched with sparkly gold.
We gather gems from crazy times,
Creating art with silly rhymes.

Together we build this quirky scene,
Celebrating all the in-between.
Pieces fitting, oh so right,
Our crafted soul, laughter's light.

Veils of Wonder

In a sock drawer, treasures hide,
A missing earring, my cat's pride.
The rings of cereal, stacked up high,
Who knew my breakfast could bling so sly?

A salad bowl holds gems galore,
Tomato necklaces we all adore.
With lettuce leaves, we craft a crown,
Only to trip while strutting 'round town!

Flipping pancakes, a golden sight,
Maple syrup sparkles just right.
With waffle earrings and toast chains near,
Breakfast fashion is truly here!

In this world where chaos sings,
My fridge is home to shiny things.
A spoon for a scepter, oh what a laugh,
Who needs real jewels? Just take a photograph!

Threads of Radiance

My grandma's threads are quite the show,
She crochets hats that steal the glow.
With mismatched yarn and colors bright,
All my friends are in for a fright!

A patchwork scarf that covers my face,
I call it 'Chic'—it's truly a race.
With errant loops that dangle and sway,
I trip on my toes and shout, "Hooray!"

Socks with holes, a daring flair,
I strut through life without a care.
They say they're 'vintage,' I buy the lie,
Who needs a fashion sense when you can fly?

So let's stitch joy with every thread,
A tapestry of laughs ahead.
Our outfits misfit, yet so divine,
In this colorful chaos, we truly shine!

Splendid Secrets

What's that under the bed, oh dear?
A shoe with a secret that's brought me cheer!
A sock puppet whispers tales so bold,
In the world of fun, it's purest gold.

Cereal boxes, hiding the loot,
A ring of peas or a banana boot!
With choices so wild, I can't sit still,
I mix and match—it's a fashion thrill!

Old Halloween costumes come alive,
A pirate hat makes me feel like a five.
With mismatched shoes and glittery wings,
I dance like no one cares for such things!

Splendid secrets in every nook,
In this treasure trove, come take a look.
For in the chaos, there lies a cue,
That fun and laughter wear funny views!

Celestial Trinkets

In the backyard, stars fall like rain,
My twinkling trinkets are so insane.
A frisbee's a planet, yes, I decree,
If you squint hard, you might see a bee!

With bottle caps shining, dear cosmic finds,
I declare that my yard's where magic unwinds.
A garden gnome wears a glittery cape,
He's the defender of my lollipop shape!

Backyards are portals to space and time,
A swing is a rocket, it's truly sublime.
With every swing upward, I reach for the stars,
In this land of laughter, we'll travel so far!

So embrace silly with every delight,
For celestial trinkets make laughter ignite.
With friends by my side, let's fly through the night,
In the galaxy of joy, everything feels right!

Ethereal Bling

In a cosmic shop, pearls float and twirl,
Diamonds giggle, watch them swirl.
An angel dropped a brooch one day,
Now it dances, 'What do you say?'

Gold chains whisper secrets at night,
While rubies blush from a fond delight.
Necklaces tease the cats that play,
'Climb aboard, we're on our way!'

Rings tickle fingers with a zing,
Bracelets jingle like they're in a swing.
With laughter strewn around each thread,
Even shadows wear a smile instead!

In this bazaar of spirits so bold,
Every gem tells a story untold.
So wear your sparkles, flaunt them high,
For even a comet loves to fly!

The Opulent Spirit

A crown of clouds upon my head,
Hats made of whispers and dreams unsaid.
I jest with jewels, dance to their tune,
A moonbeam's laugh lights up the room.

My earrings chime like curious birds,
Each twinkle provokes some laughter, absurd.
Charming cascades in shades of 'Wow!'
Even the sun can't help but bow!

Laughter's in the gems; who would have thought?
Each glimmer teases a plot I forgot.
Even the studs begin to sway,
While grinning at clouds that drift away.

In this realm where giggles reign supreme,
The opulent spirit is the wildest dream.
So strut your sparkle, let the fun unfold,
Each trinket a story, wildly bold!

Heartfelt Accessory

A brooch that hugs your heart so tight,
Grins at strangers with sheer delight.
Wearing a smile like a pearly ring,
Fashioning laughter in every swing.

Bracelets gossip, such playful friends,
Sharing secrets that never end.
With every clasp, they wink and tease,
Wear them like joy, get lost in the breeze.

Necklaces frolic, dancing in style,
They twirl and whirl with cheeky guile.
Each gem a giggle, each chain a sigh,
In the world of sparkle, let worries fly!

So necklace, brooches, come step along,
We'll host a party, where spirits belong.
With each heartfelt piece, life gets a lift,
Fashion your joy, it's the perfect gift!

Aurora of Emotions

With a dazzling dawn, the jewels awake,
In hues of giggles, the laughter will shake.
Rings of delight spin round and round,
Each shimmer a sound, a joy profound.

Gems slip and slide on a glistening rail,
Chasing the sun, they'll never fail.
With every sparkle comes a chuckle or two,
'What's that noise?' just laughter, it's true!

Brooches chuckle, while necklaces wink,
Every twist and turn makes spirits rethink.
In this parade of glimmer and glee,
Even clouds join in, 'Come dance with me!'

So let this aurora of laughter rise,
With charms on our hearts, we'll claim the skies.
Dance through the day with a heart full of shine,
In this realm of joy, we're all divine!

Crystals of Resilience

A diamond's tough, but with grease,
You'll find it shines a tad less, you see.
But with a wink and a spritz of hope,
We polish our flaws with a little more soap.

Rubies sparkle, but oh dear,
Add a bit of glitter and they disappear!
They twinkle like stars, but let's be real,
They're only as bright as our brunch-time meal.

Emeralds whisper, 'Don't stress too much,'
I laugh, they gleam: oh, life's such a crutch!
We dust off the worries, just like a chair,
And wear our humor like fine underwear.

So let us gather each colorful shard,
With laughter and joy, life's never too hard.
Embrace the chaos, wear it with pride,
In the world of bling, it's a fun roller ride.

Treasures of the Heart

In the chest of the heart, I hold my gold,
But it's mostly just memories, funny and bold.
There's a locket of laughter, a bracelet of glee,
A gem for each blooper, I cherish with glee.

A pearl for the times I slipped on my feet,
A ruby for burns from the oven, oh sweet!
With scissors and band-aids we patch up the fun,
In this treasure chest, every wound's just begun.

A brooch for each secret, I've pinned to my soul,
An anklet for joy when I'm spinning out whole.
So here goes a wink and a giggle or two,
For each silly moment, my diamonds shine through.

Let's toast to the laughter that's buried right deep,
In the vault of our hearts, it's where we can leap.
With every crack, another story unfurls,
In our box of treasures, the humor just swirls.

Adorned in Memories

A crown made of chaos, adorned with delight,
Each trouble a jewel, sparkling so bright.
I wear my mishaps like necklaces bold,
With stories of failures more precious than gold.

There's a charm for each slip, a laugh for each tear,
I twirl in my tiara of glorious fear.
Each shiny catastrophe, I wear with a grin,
In my wild wardrobe, let the madness begin!

The earrings are echoes of joy and dismay,
When I tripped on my thoughts, and then skipped on my way.
They jingle and jangle, whispering near,
"Life's flavored with funny, so let's shed a tear!"

So here's to our trinkets, our laughter entwined,
Let's dance with our baubles, unwind and unwind.
For in this sweet chaos, my spirit takes flight,
Embracing each sparkle, in day and in night.

Gems of the Spirit

The gemstones of spirit, they glow and they flash,
Like my old pair of slippers, worn down in a dash.
A sapphire for sass, I wear on my sleeve,
It's the sparkle of laughter, you wouldn't believe!

An opal of optimism, it shimmers like sun,
When life gives me lemons, I say, 'Let's have fun!'
I toss them like confetti, a fruity delight,
In the carnival of life, let our spirits take flight!

With amethyst giggles and a topaz of cheer,
We strut through the challenges, casting out fear.
For each moment a gem, whether polished or rough,
In the treasure of laughter, life's always enough.

So let's toast to our jewels, all quirky and bright,
In the necklace of being, we sparkle with might.
Our hearts hold the secrets, our spirits, the key,
In this wild game of life, just be you and be free!

The Glimmer of Being

In pockets of smiles, treasures gleam,
Whispers of laughter, a shared dream.
With a wink and a nod, we parade our flair,
Dancing with joy, without a care.

A crooked old ring, a tale comes alive,
From grandma's past, with a twist to thrive.
We trip in our jewels, yet laugh all the more,
In silly antics, our spirits soar.

Sparkles of chaos, glittering fun,
Every mishap, a story begun.
Gems of good humor, bright stars on a spree,
We wear our quirks, like fine jewelry.

So here's to the glimmers, the odd little finds,
The jewel-toned moments that life unwinds.
Each chuckle a gem that we hold up high,
In the vault of our hearts, let the laughter fly.

Stories Worn Like Gold

Draped in the memories, stories unfold,
Adventures in laughter, worth more than gold.
With mismatched earrings, we strut down the street,
Tales of mischief beneath our feet.

A bracelet of blunders, crafted with care,
Each link a bright moment, a snicker to share.
A brooch of absurdity pinned to our hearts,
We treasure the laughter that never departs.

Rings of resilience, each twist a good jest,
Worn close to the heart, they spark joy at best.
Our lives are a tapestry, woven in cheer,
With stories like gems, forever held dear.

So wear your own tale, shine bright with a grin,
The laughter we gather, our true golden skin.
In every small moment, may hilarity greet,
As we shine with the stories that make us complete.

Resplendent Echoes

In echoes of laughter, our spirits do shine,
Each chuckle a pearl, so uniquely divine.
We strut like peacocks, our colors ablaze,
In the dance of the goofy, we set hearts to praise.

Glittering gaffes turn to cherished delight,
The blunders we cherish, the wrongs that feel right.
A crown of confusion, a tiara of fun,
We sparkle with mischief, when the day is done.

Each giggle a gemstone, each snort a bright gem,
With friends as our jewels, life's a fun stem.
With laughter as our language, we play in the sun,
Resplendent echoes, and we're only half done!

So treasure those moments, with whimsy imbued,
Our laughter is gold, an eternal prelude.
As we twirl through the ages, side by side we twine,
In the laughter of being, we forever shine.

Shards of Light

In shards of bright joy, we collect our fun,
Each awkward mishap, a race that's just begun.
With a wink and a giggle, we trip through the night,
Our happiness scattered, but oh, what a sight!

A necklace of puns, so humor adorned,
Each laugh that we share, a bond newly formed.
With flash of the silly, we dazzle and spin,
In a circus of twists, where we all fit in.

A kaleidoscope of moments, reflecting our glee,
With folly like diamonds, we wear them with glee.
Each misstep a victory, each fall a good cheer,
In shards of light laughter, our souls draw near.

So gather your sparkles, let merriment thrive,
With shards of pure joy, we come alive.
In the treasure of laughter, let's all take flight,
Together we shine, in this dance of delight.

Heartfelt Adornments

A brooch made of giggles and cheer,
It sparkles like laughter, so near.
With charms of snickers, it gleams bright,
A silly dance adds to its light.

My necklace of dreams, oh what a sight,
Bling that brings joy—what a delight!
With each twist and turn, it sings,
Wearing a crown made of silly things.

Bracelets of memories, jangly and fun,
Each jingle a story, a joke not yet done.
Worn with a wink, I'm a sight to behold,
In this carnival of quirks, happiness unfolds.

So let's deck ourselves in mirthful attire,
With necklaces of jests, we'll never tire.
In the treasure hunt of giggles, we find,
The best kind of bling is all in the mind.

The Glow From Within

In my heart, a lantern shines bright,
Illuminating moments of pure delight.
With every chuckle, it flickers and sways,
Creating a glow that brightens the days.

A shimmer of mischief, oh what a glow!
Like fireflies dancing, putting on a show.
Each chuckle a beam, every snicker a ray,
Lighting up paths in the funnest way.

When worries creep in like shadows of night,
I turn up the laughter; what a sweet fight!
With hues of joy, I paint my own sky,
With a giggle as brush, oh me, oh my!

So let's shine together, all under one sun,
In this glow of ours, we'll never be done.
With twinkles and winks, let's spread the cheer,
For the brightest of lights come from hearts held dear.

A Tapestry of Light

Weaving together our moments so sweet,
Each thread is a laugh, every knot is a treat.
In this tapestry made from joy and jest,
We find that our hearts are truly blessed.

Like glittering stars in the fabric of night,
The stitches of smiles are a glorious sight.
Embroidered with giggles, sewn tight with glee,
This quilt of our life is a jolly decree.

With patches of friendship and love stitched so fine,
Every color a memory, it all aligns.
In each corner a story, so rich and absurd,
Every loop a reminder of laughter heard.

So let's wrap ourselves in this joyful expanse,
With a patch called "fun," we'll forever dance.
In this light of hilarity, we surely glow,
A tapestry made of joy is the best way to flow.

Celestial Essence

Stars in our giggles, planets in our grins,
Each comet of joy knows how to spin.
In this cosmic dance of laughter we find,
A universe of smiles, so sweet and kind.

The moon winks at us, what a hilarious sight,
As we twirl 'round the sun, our spirits take flight.
With meteors of laughter that streak through the night,
This celestial essence makes everything bright.

Dressed in smiles like constellations so bold,
Each expression a treasure, a story retold.
In this galaxy of goofiness, let's unite,
For the essence of laughter feels just so right.

So gather your stardust, let's shine evermore,
With a cosmic delight that we simply adore.
Let's drift through the cosmos, our spirits unfurl,
In the universe of joy, we create our own whirl.

Gems of the Heart

In a world so bright and bold,
Hearts are shiny, never old.
With laughter as the precious stone,
We wear our joy like a funny groan.

Collecting giggles, one by one,
Polished smiles just for fun.
Every quirk, a sparkling gem,
In this treasure hunt, we laugh at them.

When sadness tries to take a seat,
We toss it out—it's just not neat!
With puns and jokes, we ring a bell,
Our hearts shine bright, it's quite swell!

So gather 'round, let humor play,
With every chuckle, we display.
A gem-studded heart, so full of cheer,
In this glorious dance, we have no fear!

Adornments of Emotion

Life's a party, wear your grin,
With quirky hats and elbow skin.
Emotions spark like disco lights,
We twirl around on funny nights.

Our fears wrapped snug in glitter's glow,
We strut our stuff—come see the show!
Anxieties dressed in clownish wear,
Laughter's crown is what we bear.

With frilly cuffs of joy we flaunt,
Each giggle's worth a royal jaunt.
From silly dance to joking tale,
Adorned in smiles, we'll never fail.

So polish those quirks, they shine so bright,
With humor's flair, we take our flight.
In this tale, where humor roams,
We decorate our hearts as homes!

Hidden Treasures Within

Beneath the surface, snooze and dream,
Lies a treasure chest, bursting at the seam.
With silly socks and mismatched shoes,
We root for laughter; it never snooze.

Ticklish moments in secret spots,
With playful glee and tangled knots.
In awkward dances, we find the gold,
These hidden gems are bright and bold.

From silly selfies to goofy grins,
Life's perfect gems are where it begins.
With every twist of fate we know,
Treasures bloom where laughter grows.

So dive deep into this funny chest,
Where memorable moments come to rest.
In hearts adorned with whimsical glow,
We find the joys that always flow!

Radiance of the Spirit

Shining bright like a disco ball,
Our spirits dance, we have a ball.
With jokes that tickle, hearts are light,
In every giggle, spirits take flight.

Gleaming laughter, a radiant spark,
Painting the world with a funny mark.
With pun-filled chatter, we weave our cheer,
A tapestry of joy that's crystal clear.

In whimsical ways, we paint the town,
With spirit gems, we'll never frown.
For every chuckle and silly quirk,
We brighten lives, that's our work!

So lift your heart and share the grin,
Let humor's light shine from within.
With every giggle and playful cheer,
We illuminate the world, my dear!

Luminous Sentiments

In the attic, I found some beads,
A necklace made from lost old seeds.
They sparkle bright, oh what a sight,
A fashion statement—pure delight!

With buttons sewed from granddad's coat,
A quirky look, I'll surely gloat.
My friends all laugh, I twist and twine,
An outfit mixed with grandma's wine!

Glimmering Threads

A paperclip dangles on my chain,
Each piece tells stories, not mundane.
With glitter glue and a toothpick crown,
I strut around like I own the town.

Old cereal boxes make earrings new,
Frosted flakes—the world's best view!
I spin and twirl, what a grand parade,
In this bling of laughs, I've got it made!

Embers of Emotion

A heart-shaped rock from lovely streams,
Carried with care, it fuels my dreams.
Painted bright in hues so bold,
A trinket rich with stories untold.

With popsicle sticks, I make a ring,
Each laugh I wear makes my heart sing.
My friends all say, 'What a fine piece!'
In this silly joy, my soul finds peace!

Vibrant Adornments

With shoelaces tied up in knots so tight,
I sport a look that's pure delight.
A crown made of chips, oh what a scene,
Dazzling dreams in ketchup red sheen!

A jigsaw puzzle piece on my hat,
I strut proudly, and how about that?
With mismatched flair, I walk the street,
In this quirky style, life feels so sweet!

Seen and Unseen Treasures

In a box of quirky finds, a glittering piece,
Laughter blinks in the shine, the humor's never ceased.
A rubber chicken necklace, oh so delightfully bright,
Who knew fashion could be such a comical sight?

My grandma's old brooch, shaped like a cat,
Wobbles with style, imagine that!
It whispers tales of family lore,
While making everyone laugh, who could ask for more?

A sock full of bangles, a jangling parade,
Every step I take, it's a symphonic charade.
Dancing with joy, I twirl and I caper,
My jewelry box is the ultimate paper!

The treasures we wear, both silly and sweet,
With a wink and a grin, we can't be beat.
Embellishments spark joy, a fun-loving rule,
Who knew life's a party, it's pearls in a pool?

Spirited Ornaments

A bracelet of fidget spinners, a whirlwind of flair,
Each twist and turn spills giggles in the air.
With every little twinkle, joy does unfold,
Ornaments of spirit, never grown old!

Earrings like marshmallows, fluffy and round,
Each jingle and jangle, laughter is found.
Whispers of whimsy in every small blink,
Jewels of humor, give us time to think!

A tiara of tacos, for the queen of fun,
Crowned with delight, oh, isn't she the one?
Life's festive adornments, kooky but true,
In this cavalcade of sparkle, we dance anew!

From pearls of giggles to charms of cheer,
We wear our quirks proudly, with nothing to fear.
Together we shine, a colorful bunch,
With spirited trinkets, life's a grand brunch!

Timeless Gleam

In the attic, a treasure, a necklace of bells,
Every jingle a story, where laughter dwells.
A timepiece that wobbles and plays silly tunes,
With moments like this, we laugh at the moons!

A crown of bright stickers, stuck on with glee,
Adorning my head like, 'Look at me!'
Timeless yet tacky, what's not to adore?
It's a reminder that joy is worth more!

Rings of odd colors, each one a vibe,
Worn on my fingers, they dance and they jibe.
With a wink at the world, I jest and I beam,
In the treasure of life, there's always a theme!

Shiny reflections, a giggling glow,
With jewels of laughter, we steal the show.
Cascading through moments, our spirits take flight,
In a world full of gems, we delight in the light!

Echoes in Gemstone

Echoes of laughter, like gems by the sea,
I wear my bizarre trinkets, wild and free.
A choker of spaghetti, it swings with a twirl,
Biting into laughter, watch the chaos unfurl!

In a shimmering bracelet, a dance of the fries,
Each jolt and each wiggle brings tears to the eyes.
Bejeweled with humor, a crown made of cheese,
How could I resist such whimsical tease?

A brooch shaped like bacon, I flaunt without shame,
In this world of odd jewels, who needs a lame name?
Gloriously goofy, I strut about town,
With echoes of giggles, I'll never frown!

So let's celebrate life with these quirky delights,
In necklaces laden with laughter-filled nights.
Our ornaments shine, making memories glean,
In the treasure of humor, forever we're keen!

The Luster of Life

In pockets stuffed with shiny things,
A fortune made of rubber rings.
We wear our joys like bright beets,
With silly hats and funky feet.

Every laugh, a shiny bead,
Each mishap, something we don't need.
We twirl in circles, all askew,
Life's a dance, now, laugh with me too!

With every funny face we mold,
Our spirits shine like polished gold.
For what's a crown without a jest?
In this grand circus, we're the best!

So let's adorn with mirth and glee,
Each giggle sparkles—can't you see?
In every chuckle, pure delight,
We're precious gems, oh, what a sight!

Shining Prisms

A rainbow's twirl across the room,
With silly socks, we chase the gloom.
We build our castles made of fun,
With wobbly chairs, we've all but won!

Our laughter bounces off the walls,
Like shiny marbles, it enthralls.
In every joke, a prism shines,
Colors of joy, like playful lines.

With each delight, a glimmer bends,
Like buddies spinning, never ends.
Our little quirks, they sparkle bright,
We're all just prisms in the light!

Let's prance like peacocks, silly, bold,
In the warmth of friendships, we find gold.
Chasing giggles, we twirl and sway,
In this kaleidoscope, we play!

Essence in Veils

Behind our smiles, oh what a mask,
A playful secret, what a task!
We dance with glee beneath the stars,
Hiding giggles, beneath our scars.

With silly wigs and quirky hats,
We flaunt our charms like curious cats.
In every twist, a truth shines bright,
A joyous heart in every sight!

Veils of laughter spin around,
Every tumble is joy unbound.
We wear our quirks with bold embrace,
Each giggle etched upon our face.

Behind the curtain, we will play,
In this farce of life, let joy relay.
For in the layers, we discover,
The light within, a lovely cover!

Gemstones of the Mind

In minds like treasure chests, we play,
With thoughts that sparkle every day.
A wacky world, where giggles twine,
Like sparkling gems, we intertwine.

Our brain's a mine of silly tales,
Where every thought like humor sails.
A glint of wit, a shine of fun,
In goofy dreams, we all have won!

With every quip, a diamond gleams,
In laughter's light, we chase our dreams.
So let your mind shine bold and free,
In this gem-studded jubilee!

For every jest, a treasure found,
In friendship's vault, we're tightly wound.
So raise your glass and toast it loud,
To lands of laughter, we're all proud!

www.ingramcontent.com/pod-product-compliance
Lightning Source LLC
Chambersburg PA
CBHW060110230426
43661CB00003B/138